24-105mm 1:4

LENS

Ø77mm

Australia

the land down under

Contents

Sydney's iconic Opera House and the city skyline

New South Wales

Sydney Opera House, Sydney

Luna Park and the Sydney Harbour Bridge, Sydney

Luna Park, Sydney

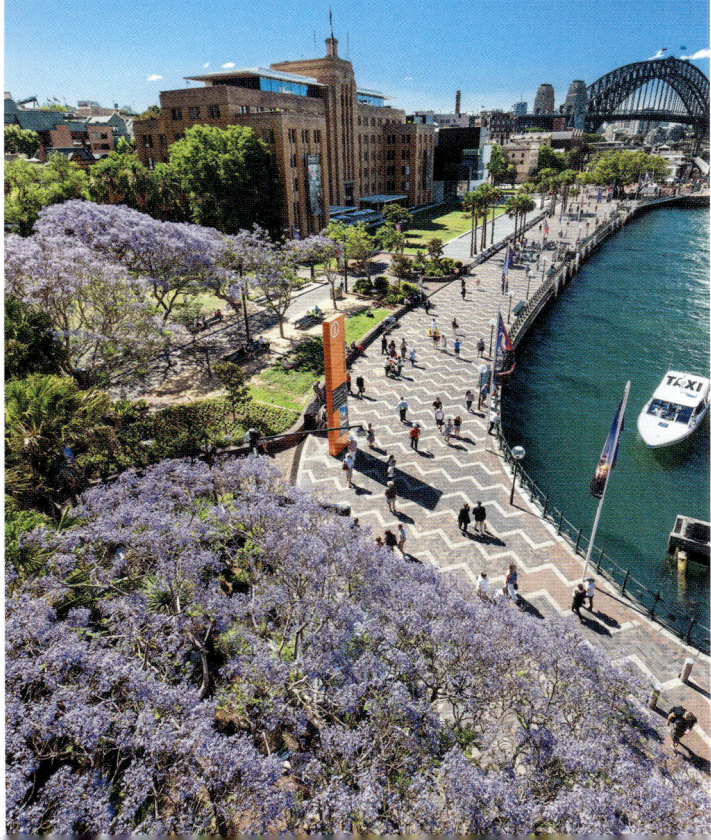

View of Circular Quay
and the Museum of
Contempray Art, Sydney

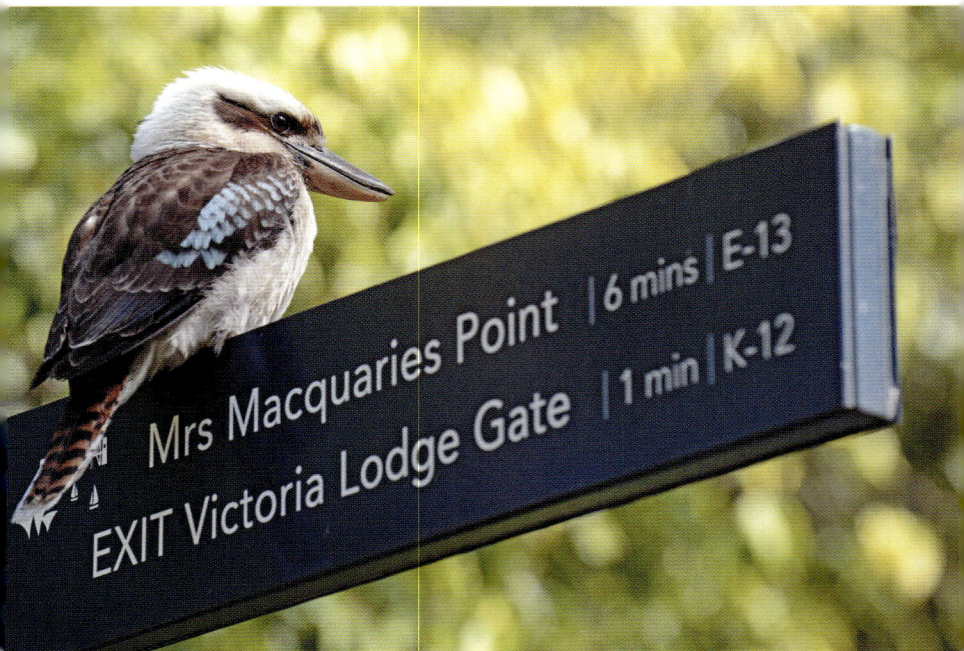

Mrs Macquaries Point | 6 mins | E-13

EXIT Victoria Lodge Gate | 1 min | K-12

Royal Botanic Gardens, Sydney

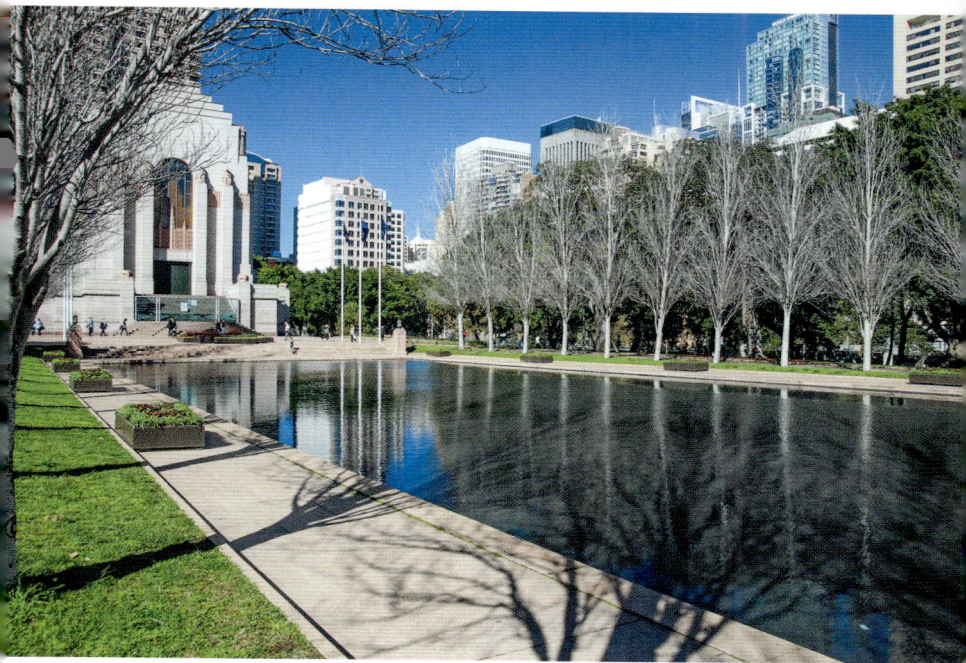

ANZAC Memorial, Hyde Park, Sydney

The Archibald Fountain with St Mary's Cathedral in the background, Hyde Park, Sydney

St Mary's Cathedral, Sydney

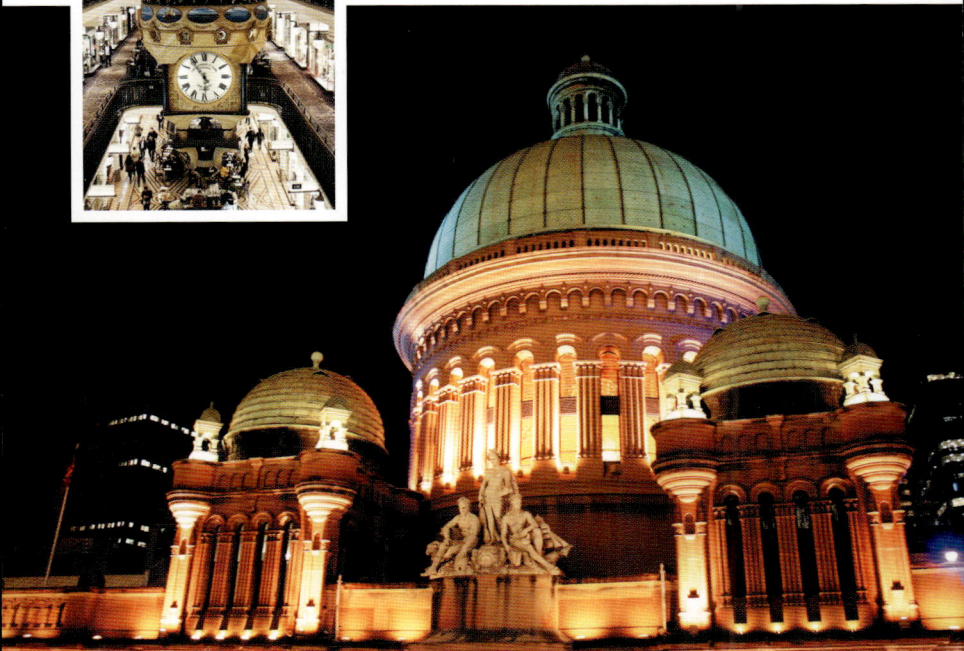

Queen Victoria Building, Sydney

Emu, koala, crocodile and lions at
Taronga Zoo, Sydney

Bondi Beach, Sydney

Giraffes at Taronga Zoo, Sydney

The Three Sisters, Blue Mountains National Park

Jenolan Caves, Blue Mountains National Park

Treetop Adventure Park, Wyong

A vineyard, Hunter Valley

Humpback whale, Coffs Harbour

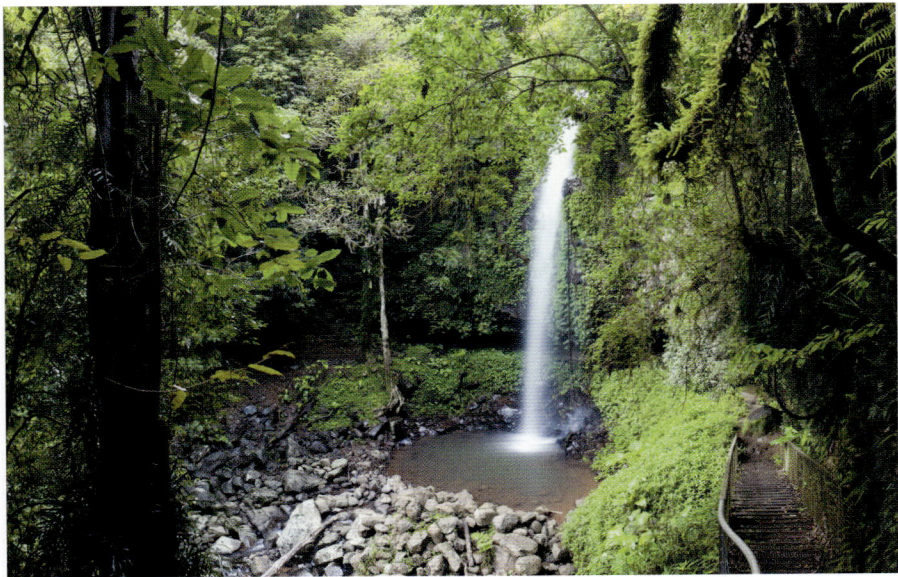

Crystal Shower Falls, Dorrigo National Park

Cape Byron Lighthouse, Byron Bay

Grass trees, Warrumbungle National Park

Honeymoon Bay, Jervis Bay Territory **INSET** Seal, Eurobodalla

A snow gum tree, Snowy Mountains

Skiing, Snowy Mountains

The Living Desert Reserve, near Broken Hill

Aerial view of Canberra

Australian Capital Territory

Parliament House, Canberra

Australian War Memorial, Canberra

Lake Burley Griffin, Canberra

Museum of Australian Democracy at Old Parliament House, Canberra

National Gallery of Australia, Canberra

National Carillon, Canberra

National Library of Australia, Canberra

RIGHT National Museum of Australia, Canberra

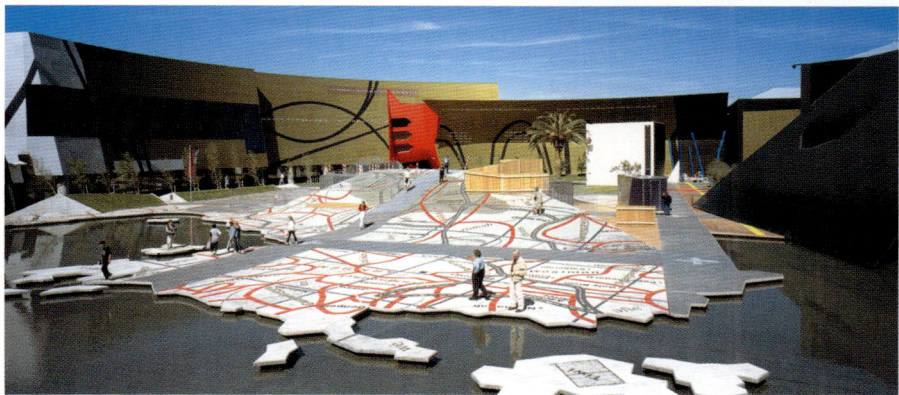

NASA's Deep Space Communication Complex, Tidbinbilla

Corin Dam, Tidbinbilla

Melbourne's city skyline

Victoria

Flinders Street Station, Melbourne

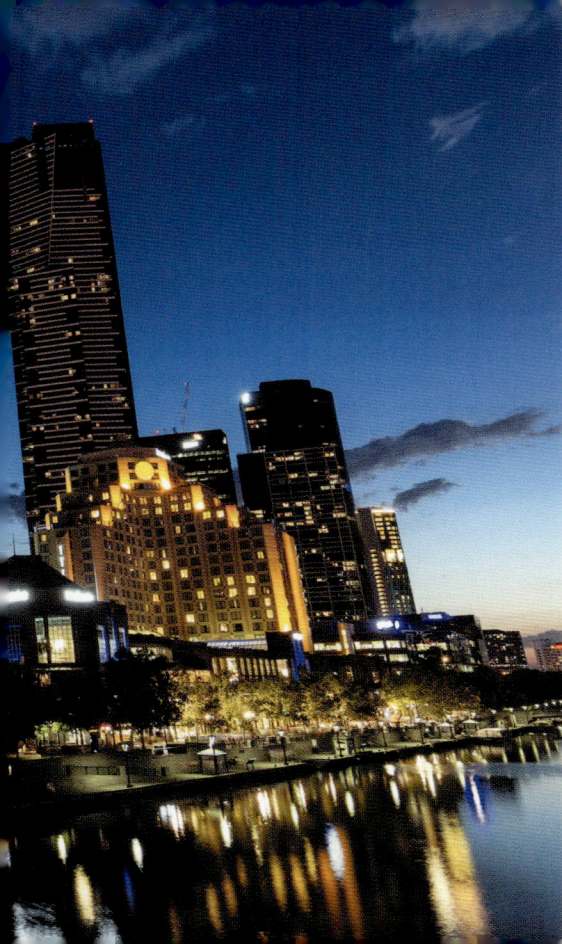

Southgate and the arts precinct, Melbourne

Eureka Tower, Melbourne

Vintage tram, Melbourne

National Gallery of Victoria (NGV), Melbourne

The Arts Centre spire, Melbourne

The Shrine of Remembrance, Melbourne

Fitzroy Gardens, Melbourne

Federation Square, Melbourne

The Princess Theatre, Melbourne

Interior of The Regent
Theatre, Melbourne

The Shot Tower inside Melbourne Central, Melbourne

Nicholas Building, Melbourne

Webb Bridge, Docklands, Melbourne

Melbourne Star, Docklands, Melbourne

Bathing boxes, Brighton Beach, Melbourne

Puffing Billy steam train, the Dandenongs

The Black Spur, Yarra Valley

Yarra Ranges National Park, Yarra Valley

Hot-air ballooning over vineyards, Yarra Valley

Wilsons Promontory, Gippsland **INSET** Wombat, Wilsons Promontory, Gippsland

Croajingolong National Park, East Gippsland

Ballarat, Goldfields

Bendigo, Goldfields

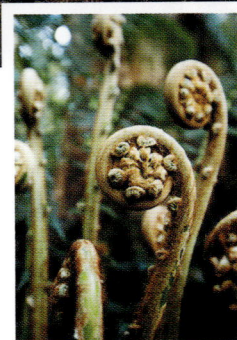

Great Otway National Park, South-West

The Great Ocean Road, South-West

The Twelve Apostles, Great Ocean Road

The Great Ocean Walk

Grampians National Park, the Grampians

Halls Gap, the Grampians

Lake Mountain, High Country

Mount Buller, High Country

Murray River

Sunset, Adelaide Hills

South Australia

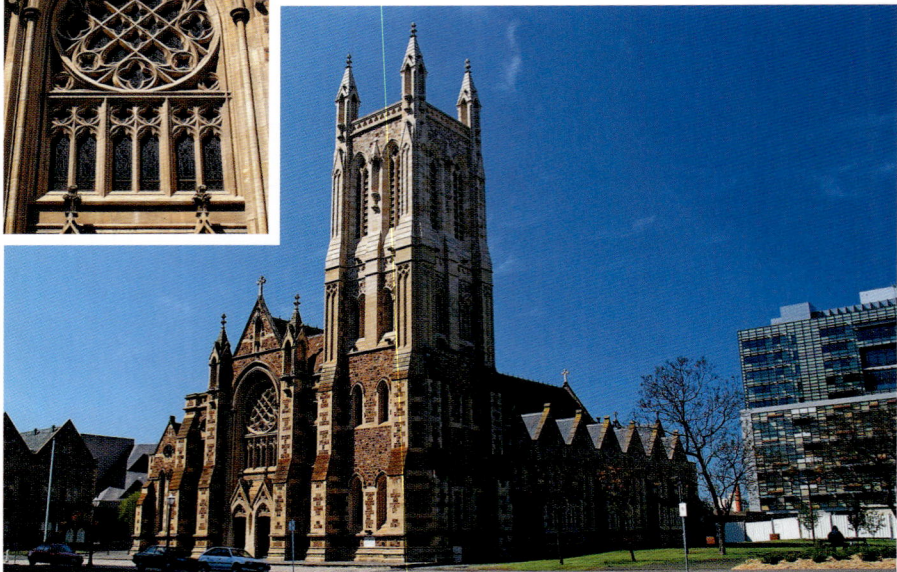

St Francis Xavier Cathedral, Adelaide

State Library of South Australia, Adelaide

Elder Hall, Adelaide

Rotunda at Elder Park, Adelaide

Fountain near Elder Park, in River Torrens, Adelaide

Adelaide Zoo, Adelaide

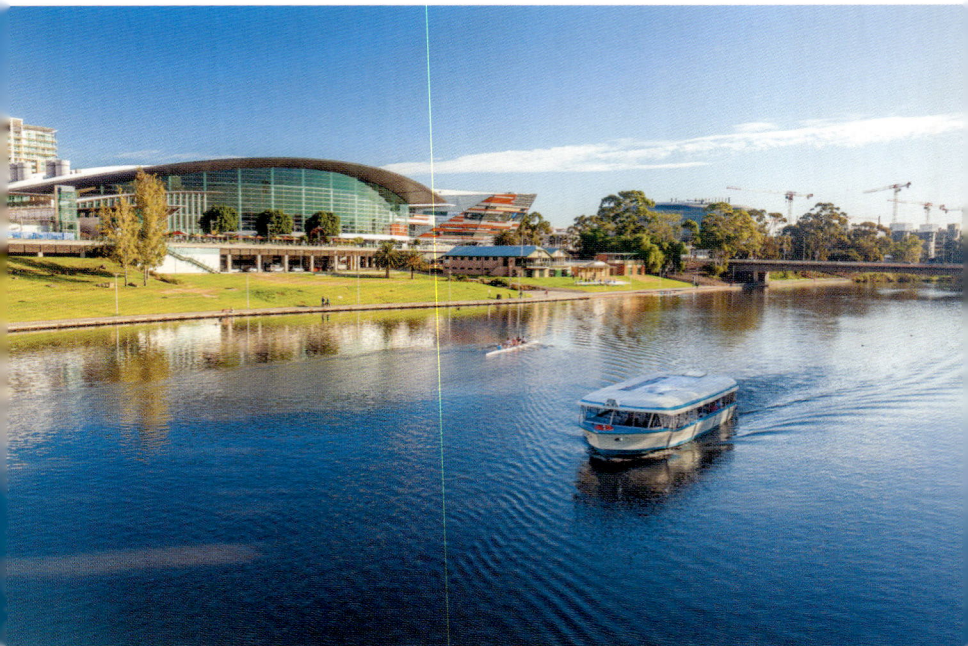

View of Adelaide from River Torrens, Adelaide

HMS *Buffalo*, Adelaide

Glenelg Town Hall, Adelaide

Sunrise at Grange Beach, Adelaide

Wine barrels, Barossa Valley

Sunset over a vineyard, Barossa Valley

Innes National Park, Yorke Peninsula

Stenhouse Bay, Innes National Park, Yorke Peninsula

Naracoorte Caves National Park, Limestone Coast

Blue Lake, Mount Gambier, Limestone Coast

The 1852 Robe Obelisk, Limestone Coast

Wilpena Pound, Flinders Ranges National Park, Flinders Ranges

Sturt's desert pea, Flinders Ranges

Flinders Ranges

Dolphin and whale, Eyre Peninsula

Murphy's Haystacks, Eyre Peninsula

Kangaroos, Kangaroo Island

Sea lions, Kangaroo Island

Cape du Couedic Lighthouse, Kangaroo Island

Remarkable Rocks, Kangaroo Island

Sunset near Derby, The Kimberley

Western Australia

City skyline, Perth

Swan Bell Tower, Perth

Lotterywest Federation Walkway, Kings Park and Botanic Gardens, Perth

State War Memorial Cenotaph, Kings Park and Botanic Gardens, Perth

Cottesloe Beach, Perth

Coastline, Rottnest Island **INSET** Quokkas, Rottnest Island

Sunrise over vineyard, Margaret River

Busselton Jetty, near Margaret River

Karri forest, Leeuwin–Naturaliste National Park

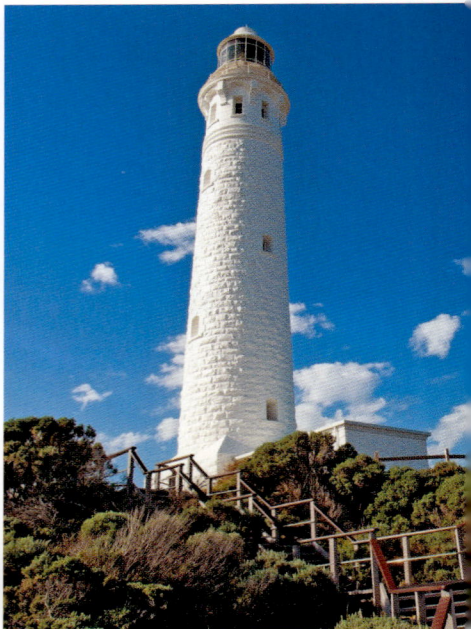

TOP LEFT Cape Naturaliste Lighthouse, Leeuwin–Naturaliste National Park **TOP RIGHT** Cape Leeuwin Lighthouse, Leeuwin–Naturaliste National Park

Tree Top Walk, Valley of the Giants, Walpole–Nornalup National Park

Conspicuous Beach near Walpole

The Pinnacles Desert, Nambung National Park

King George Falls, Kimberley

Whale shark, yellow boxfish and turtles, Ningaloo Reef

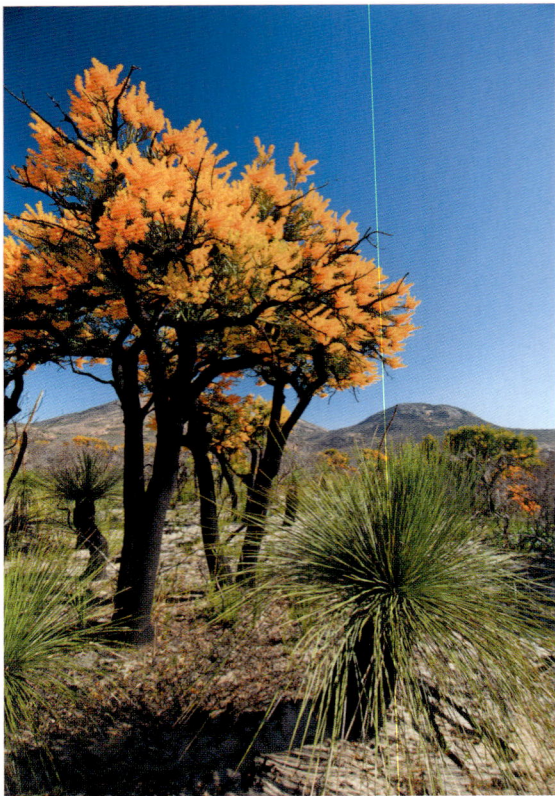

Western Australian Christmas trees, Cape Le Grand National Park

Antony Gormley sculptures, Lake Ballard

Great Southern Rail Pacific Train, Nullarbor

Nullarbor cliffs, Nullarbor

Cockburn Range, El Questro Station

Cable Beach, Broome

Wildflowers, Karijini National Park

The Bungle Bungles, Purnululu National Park

Uluṟu, the Red Centre

Northern Territory

Aerial view of Darwin

Crocosaurus Cove, Darwin

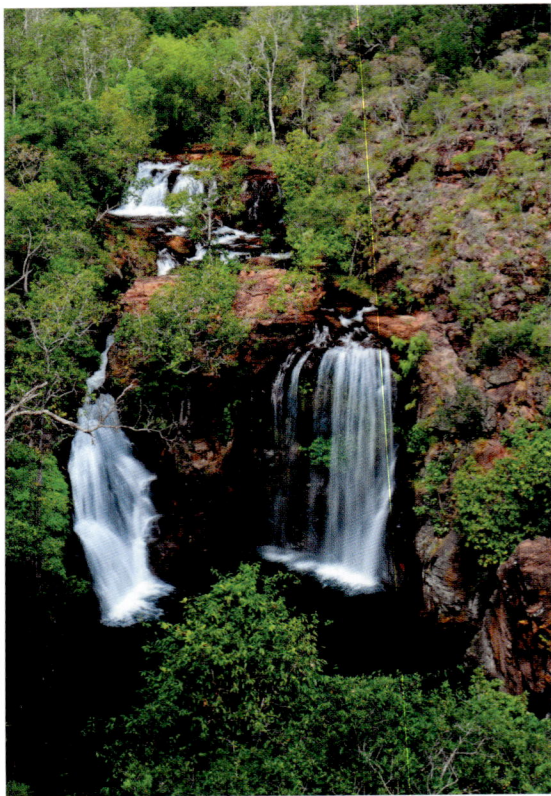

Florence Falls, Litchfield National Park, near Darwin

Mindil Beach, Darwin

Black Point, Garig Gunak Barlu National Park

Lost City, Cape Crawford

Pink lotus flowers, Kakadu National Park

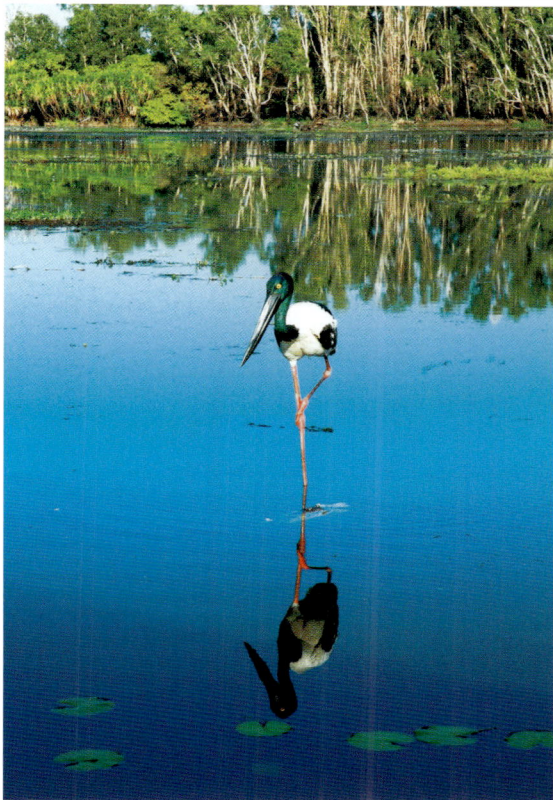

Jabiru, Yellow Water Billabong, Kakadu National Park

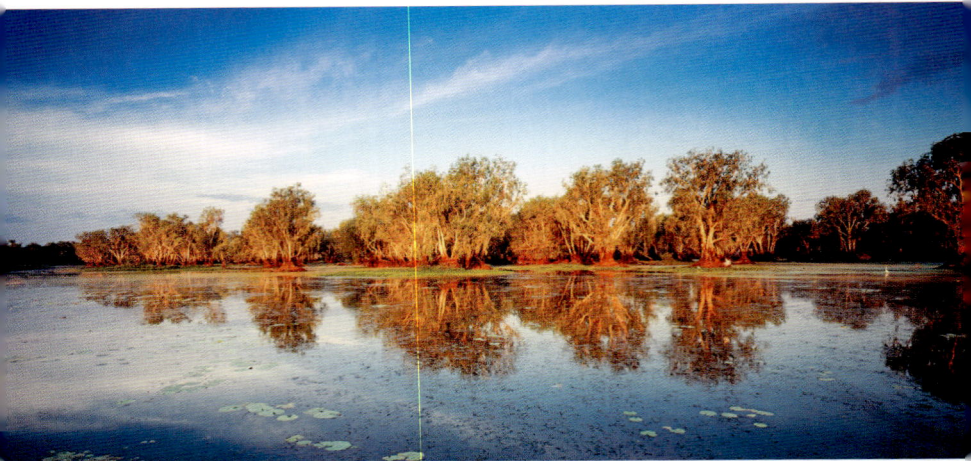

Yellow Water Billabong, Kakadu National Park

Gunlom Falls, Kakadu National Park

Judbarra–Gregory National Park

Katherine Gorge, Nitmiluk National Park

Kata Tjuṯa, Uluṟu–Kata Tjuṯa National Park

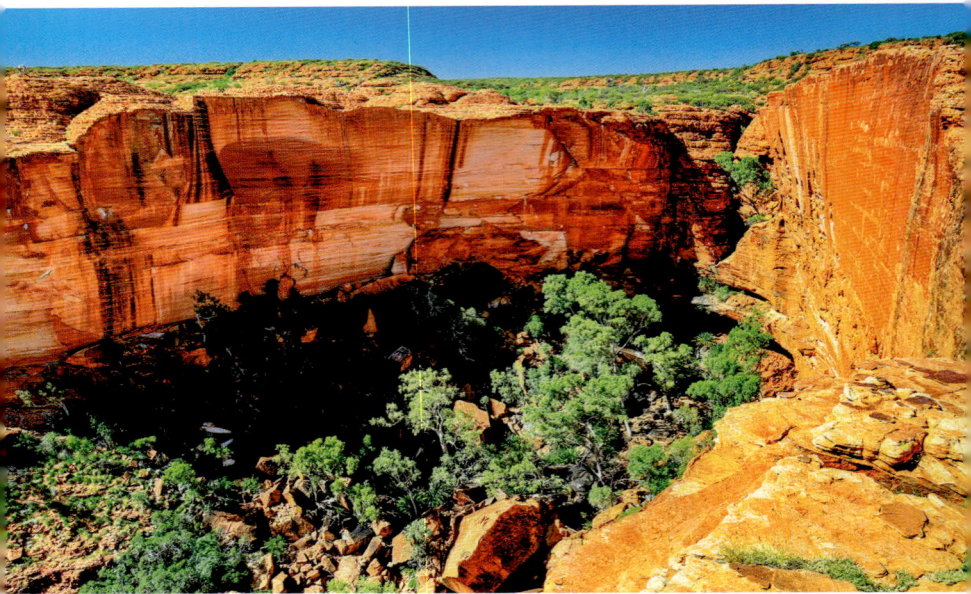

Kings Canyon, Watarrka National Park

Devils Marbles, Karlu Karlu–Devils Marbles Conservation Park

Chambers Pillar, Simpson Desert

Uluṟu–Kata Tjuṯa National Park

Surfing at sunrise, Gold Coast

Queensland

Aerial view of Brisbane

Treasury Casino, Brisbane

Nepalese pagoda, South Bank, Brisbane

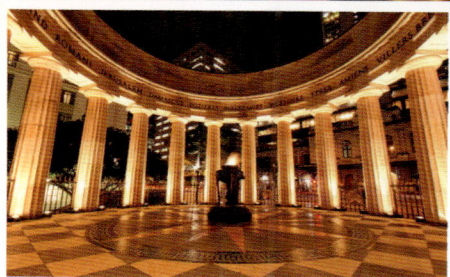

War memorial at ANZAC Square, Brisbane

Brisbane Botanic Gardens, Mt Coot-tha, Brisbane

Story Bridge, Brisbane

Manly boat harbour, Brisbane

Cape Moreton, Brisbane

Dreamworld, Gold Coast

Sea World, Gold Coast

Springbrook National Park

Mt Barney, Mount Barney National Park

Beaches, Gold Coast

Surfers Paradise, Gold Coast

Seventy Five Mile Beach, Fraser Island

SS *Maheno* shipwreck, Fraser Island

Carnarvon National Park

Off Lady Elliot Island

Kookaburras, Rockhampton **INSET** Koalas, Townsville

Planet Downs

Whitehaven Beach, Whitsundays

The Great Barrier Reef

Daintree Rainforest

Australian Stockman's Hall of Fame, Longreach

View towards Hobart from Mount Wellington

Tasmania

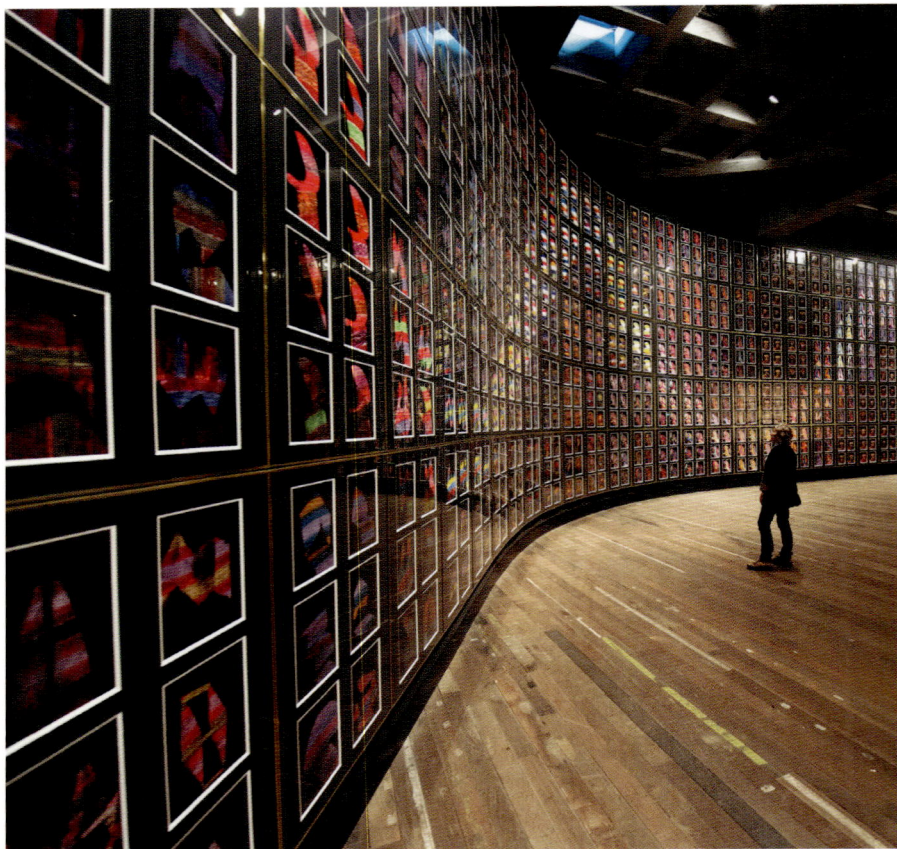

MONA (Museum of Old and New Art), Hobart

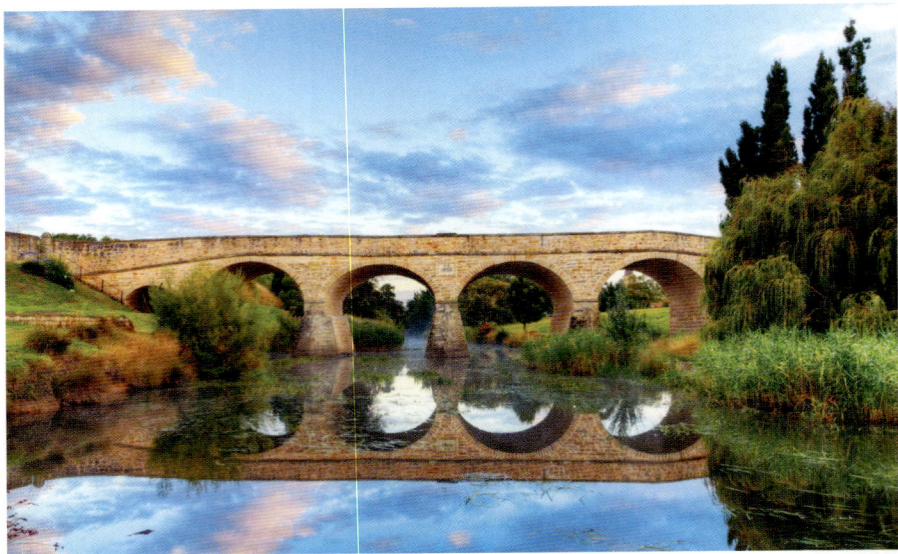

Historic Richmond Bridge, Richmond, near Hobart

Port Arthur, Tasman Peninsula

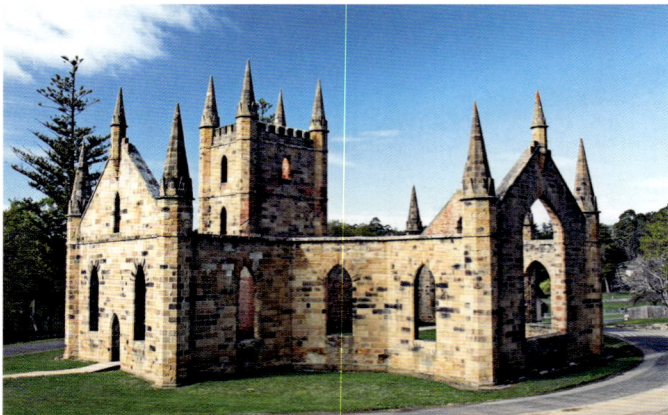

Port Arthur, Tasman Peninsula

Painted Cliffs, Maria Island National Park

Echidna, Maria Island National Park

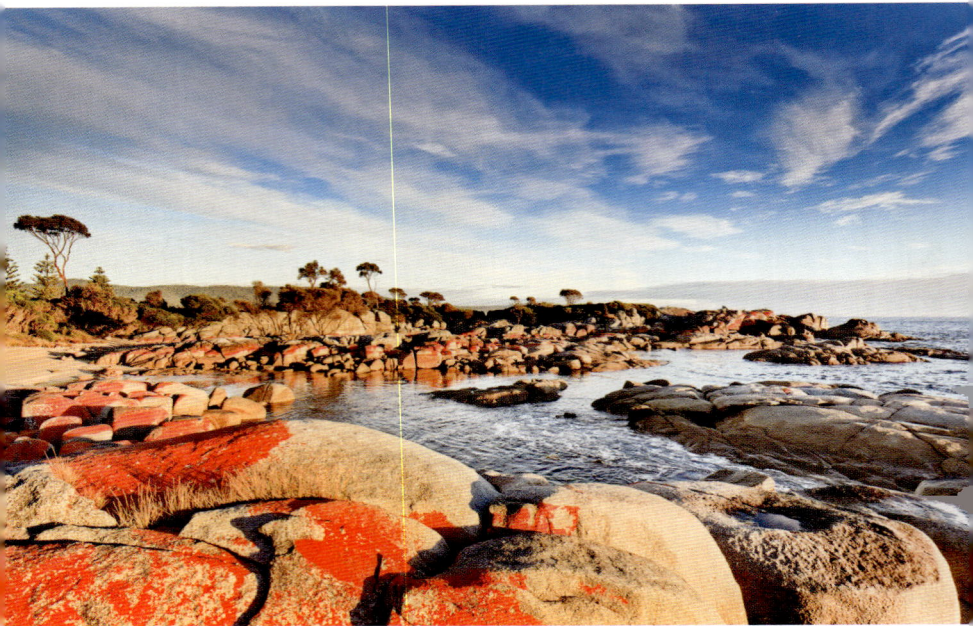

Binalong Bay, Bay of Fires

Wineglass Bay, Freycinet National Park

Vineyard, Tamar Valley

Franklin–Gordon Wild Rivers National Park

Russell Falls, Mount Field
National Park

Overland Track, Cradle Mountain–Lake St Clair National Park

Dove Lake, Cradle Mountain–Lake St Clair National Park

Cradle Mountain and Barn Bluff,
Cradle Mountain–Lake St Clair
National Park

Image acknowledgements

COVER Camera lens (©iStockphoto.com/
mariusFM77)

BACK COVER Camera viewfinder
(Matt Valentine/SH), Sydney Opera House
(Chris Howey/SH)

OTHER PAGES:
NSW

Pages iv–1 siwawut/SH; 2 DNSW; 3 Kiyoshi
Hijiki/SH; 4–5 & 6 (a) Aleksandar Todorovic/SH,
6 (b) Tooykrub/SH; 7 Hamilton Lund/DNSW;
8 robert cicchetti/SH; 9 eXpose/SH; 10 xc/SH;
11 Gordon Bell/SH; 12–13 Holli/SH; 14 (a)
Ozphotoguy/SH, (b) Dropu/SH; 15 (a) Passion
Images/SH, (b) Connie Puntoriero/SH; 16 (a)
Mandy Creighton/SH, (b) Hank Shiffman/SH;
17 (a) Kathryn Willmott/SH, (b) Mark Higgins/
SH; 18 Ethan Rohloff/DNSW; 19 DNSW;
20–21 Aleksandar Todorovic/SH; 22 Claudio
Bertoloni/SH; 23 e X p o s e/SH; 24 DNSW;
25 Murray Vanderveer/DNSW; 26 Coffs Coast
Marketing/DNSW; 27 Hamilton Lund/DNSW;
28 ian woolcock/SH; 29 Susan Wright/DNSW;
30–31 Jervis Bay Wild/DNSW, (inset) Jonathan
Poyner/DNSW; 32 Paul Sinclair/DNSW; 33 (a)
& (b) Perisher/DNSW; 34–35 Maxime Coquard/
DNSW;

ACT

36–37 VisitCanberra; 38–39 & 40 Dan
Breckwoldt/SH; 41 Inavan Hateren/SH, (inset)
EyeofPaul/SH; 42–43, 44, 45 & 46 VisitCanberra;
47 Liv Falvey/SH; 48, 49 (a) & (b) VisitCanberra;
50 Full Bottle/SH; 51 VisitCanberra;

VIC

52–53 Aleksandar Todorovic/SH; 54 (a) Neale
Cousland/SH, (b) www.harleyrides.com.au/
John Karmouche/TV; 55 Michael William/SH;
56–57 gnoparus/SH; 58 (a) ChameleonsEye/
SH, (b) TV; 59 Neale Cousland/SH; 60 Nils
Versemann/SH; 61 Jason Patrick Ross/
SH; 62 Boyloso/SH; 63 (a), (b) & (c) TV;
64 Tooykrub/SH; 65 Neale Cousland/SH;
66 & 67 TV; 68 Neale Cousland/SH; 69 (a) &
(b) TV; 70 Robyn Mackenzie/SH; 71 & (inset)
Melbourne Star Observation Wheel/TV;
72–73 Aleksandar Todorovic/SH; 74 TV;
75 Robyn Mackenzie/SH; 76 & 77 TV;
78 THPStock/SH, (inset) Robyn Butler/SH;
79 TV; 80 & (inset) TV; 81 TV; 82 CAN
BALCIOGLU/SH, (inset) TV; 83 TV; 84 idiz/SH;
85 TV; 86 (a) & (b), 87 TV; 88 FiledIMAGE/SH;
89 Roberto Seba/TV; 90–91 TV;

SA

92–93 kwest/SH; 94 & (inset) Timothy Craig Lubcke/SH; 95 & 96 SATC; 97 & 98 amophoto.net/SH; 99 (a) Cloudia Spinner/SH, (b) Ekaterina Kamenetsky/SH; 100 ymgerman/SH; 101 SATC; 102 Neale Cousland/SH; 103 trappy76/SH; 104 & 105 kwest/SH; 106 SATC; 107 ian woolcock/SH; 108 ymgerman/SH; 109 & 110 ian woolcock/SH; 111, 112 & 113 SATC; 114 (a) SATC, (b) John White Photos/SH; 115 SATC; 116 K.A.Willis/SH; 117 (a) Stephen B. Goodwin, (b) SATC; 118 Leah Kennedy/SH; 119 CSLD/SH;

WA

120–121 MelBrackstone/SH; 122 Neale Cousland/SH; 123 (a) Nokuro/SH, (b) & (c) TWA; 124 TWA; 125 imagevixen/SH; 126 David Steele/SH; 127 & (inset) TWA; 128 Kaneos Media/SH, (inset) TWA; 129 Janelle Lugge/SH; 130 (a) Gordon Bell/SH, (b) Neale Cousland/SH; 131 metriognome/SH; 132 (a) TWA, (b) Marcelle Miriello/SH; 133 Jean Leggat/TWA; 134–135 Greg Snell/TWA; 136 (a) TWA, (b) Air Images/SH; 137 Richard Rogers/SH; 138 & 139 (a) TWA, (b) Georgia Arcidiancono/TWA, (c) Greg Snell/TWA; 140 & 141 TWA; 142 Great Southern Rail/TWA; 143 TWA; 144 TWA; 145 Summer Day/TWA, (inset) Greg Snell/TWA; 146 Zeljko Radojko/SH; 147 TWA;

NT

148–149, 150 & 151 TNT; 152 Stanislav Fosenbauer/SH; 153 Will Parker/SH; 154 Pete Eve/TNT; 155 Pete Eve/TNT, (inset) TNT; 156 Peerawat Aupala; 157 TNT; 158 Janelle Lugge/SH; 159 Peter Eve/SH; 160 & 161 TNT; 162 Stanislav Fosenbauer/SH; 163 Wesley Walker/SH; 164 Stanislav Fosenbauer/SH; 165 & 166 TNT; 167 Stanislav Fosenbauer/SH;

QLD

168–169 sw_photo/SH; 170 Ethan Rohloff Photography/TEQ; 171 TEQ; 172 Steven Bostock/SH; 173 David Bostock/SH, (inset) Rob d/SH; 174 TEQ; 175 David Bostock/SH; 176, 177 & 178 TEQ; 179 (a) & (b) ChameleonsEye/SH; 180 & 181 TEQ; 182 DAE Photo/SH, (inset) Brenda Linskey/SH; 183 Jodie Nash/SH; 184–185 zstock/SH; 186 Darren Jew/TEQ; 187 Troy Wegman/SH; 188 TEQ; 189 Eddie Safarik/TEQ; 190, (inset) & 191 TEQ; 192 Tanya Puntti/SH; 193 (a) Brian Kinney/SH, (b) Tanya Puntti/SH; 194 (a) TEQ, (b) Hugh Lansdown/SH, (c) Dirk Ercken/SH; 195 TEQ;

TAS

196–197 Ellenor Argyropoulos/SH; 198 Joe McNally/TA; 199 MONA/TA; 200 Steve Daggar/SH; 201 Port Arthur Historic site Management Authority/TA; 202 (a) Neale Cousland/SH, (b) & 203 Rob Bayer/SH; 204 & 205 Maria Island Walk/Great Walks of Australia/TA; 206 Taras Vyshnya/SH; 207 & 208–209 TA; 210 ian woolcock/SH; 211 lunatix/SH; 212 urbancowboy/SH; 213 FiledIMAGE/SH; 214–215 urbancowboy/SH; 216 Anton Balazh/SH

ABBREVIATIONS

DNSW – Destination New South Wales
SATC – South Australia Tourism Commission
SH – Shutterstock.com
TA – Tourism Australia
TEQ – Tourism and Events Queensland
TNT – Tourism Northern Territory
TV – Tourism Victoria
TWA – Tourism Western Australia
VC – Visit Canberra

Acknowledgements

The publisher would like to acknowledge the following
individuals and organisations:

Project manager and editor
Alison Proietto

Editorial assistants
Anna Collett, Helena Holmgren

Cover and prelims design
Vaughan Mossop

Internal page design and layout
Megan Ellis

Pre-press
Megan Ellis, Splitting Image

Explore Australia Publishing Pty Ltd
Ground Floor, Building 1, 658 Church Street,
Richmond, VIC 3121

Explore Australia Publishing Pty Ltd is a division of
Hardie Grant Publishing Pty Ltd

hardie grant publishing

Published by Explore Australia Publishing Pty Ltd, 2015

Concept, form and design © Explore Australia Publishing
Pty Ltd, 2015

A Cataloguing-in-Publication entry is available from
the catalogue of the National Library of Australia at
www.nla.gov.au

ISBN-13 9781741175004

10 9 8 7 6 5 4 3 2 1

Printed and bound in China by 1010 Printing
International Ltd

Publisher's note: Every effort has been made to ensure
that the information in this book is accurate at the
time of going to press. The publisher welcomes
information and suggestions for correction or
improvement. Email: info@exploreaustralia.net.au

Publisher's disclaimer: The publisher cannot accept
responsibility for any errors or omissions. The publisher
cannot be held responsible for any injury, loss or damage
incurred during travel. It is vital to research any proposed
trip thoroughly and seek the advice of relevant state and
travel organisations before you leave.

www.exploreaustralia.net.au
Follow us on Twitter: @ExploreAus
Find us on Facebook: www.facebook.com/exploreaustralia